THE MOU

A selection of classic Australian poetry with contemporary Australian photography

PRINCIPAL PHOTOGRAPHY
John Meier

ADDITIONAL PHOTOGRAPHY
Peter Jarver
Carolyn Johns
Philip Quirk
Peter Solness
Grenville Turner

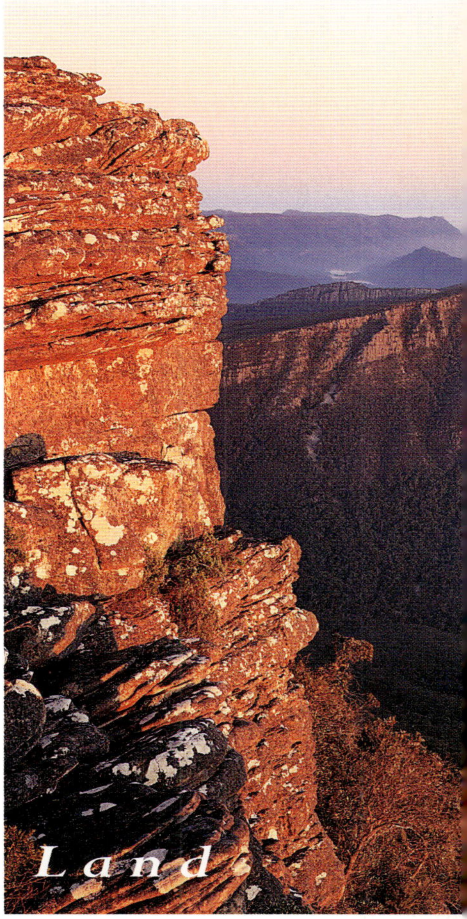

Spirit of the Land

Angus&Robertson
An imprint of HarperCollins*Publishers*

AUSTRALIAN POETS' BIOGRAPHIES

CHRISTOPHER BRENNAN 1870–1932

Christopher Brennan's Irish immigrant parents tried to encourage their son to enter the priesthood, but he was destined for a life of academia, and studied Classics and philosophy at the University of Sydney. He was later responsible for introducing into the Australian poetry scene literary influences which had interested him during his travels throughout Europe.

ADA CAMBRIDGE 1844–1926

Ada Cambridge travelled from England to Australia in 1870 with her husband, a clergyman. She wrote mostly novels, but published her first book of poetry anonymously and withdrew it shortly after, fearing that as a clergyman's wife, her independent viewpoint on religion and society might not meet with public understanding.

VICTOR DALEY 1858–1905

Though working at various times in his life as a clerk, a newspaper freelancer and an unsuccessful gold prospector, Daley mostly attempted to live by his writing, and as a consequence he often suffered poverty. As well as the poetry published under his own name, he also wrote social commentary under the name of Creeve Roe.

GEORGE ESSEX EVANS 1863–1909

English by birth, George Essex Evans emigrated to the Darling Downs in Queensland as a young man to start a new life as a farmer. He later went on to be a teacher, a public servant and to work in newspapers. A prolific poet, Evans is known for his patriotism and for his great sympathy and admiration for the early pioneers in Australia.

ADAM LINDSAY GORDON 1833–1870

While Gordon received some critical acclaim during his lifetime, he only gained wide acceptance following his suicide due to his inability to cover the printing costs of his last book of poetry. He had suffered melancholia for several years and though he had some success as a politician and horseman, he had also experienced publishing and business failures. A commemorative bust of Gordon was installed in Westminster Abbey, London, after his death.

CHARLES HARPUR 1813–1868

Charles Harpur, the son of convicts who had been emancipated by Governor Macquarie, worked as a postal clerk, a schoolteacher, a sheep farmer, and a gold commissioner for the government. He saw himself foremost as a poet though, and indeed was the first Australian-born poet to come to prominence.

EMILIE MANNING HERON ("AUSTRALIE") 1845–1890

As well as writing poetry, Heron was also a journalist and contributed to several British and Australian publications, including the *Sydney Morning Herald* and the *Illustrated Sydney News*. A strong advocate for women's access to higher education, her work was published under the name "Australie".

HENRY KENDALL 1839–1882

Henry Kendall's life was marked by both great success and hardship. Despite such promising signs as first being published at the age of 15 and winning several poetry prizes, he did experience some publishing failures. Though he was unable to fulfill his dream of abandoning routine work to concentrate solely on writing, he left behind a substantial body of work.

HENRY LAWSON 1867–1922

Though he was born in a tent on a goldfield in rural New South Wales and has a reputation as a bush poet, Henry Lawson spent most of his life in the city. Forays into the bush, and memories of his early life in the country inspired much of Lawson's writing, both poetry and short stories. One of Australia's best known writers, he was nurtured early in his career by his mother Louisa who published his poems in her own publications.

LOUISA LAWSON 1848–1920

Publishing only one book of poetry, Louisa Lawson concentrated her energies on social reform. She set up the journal *The Republican* and later *Dawn*, the first Australian magazine catering solely to women's interests. She also helped establish the Dawn Club which was active in the women's suffrage movement. She was the mother of the well-known writer, Henry Lawson.

JOHN SHAW NEILSON 1872–1942

Lacking a formal education, and constantly dogged by poverty, Neilson found a voice as a lyric poet while travelling Australia seeking work. The son of a poet who had fallen on hard times, he spent most of his life as a labourer – shearer, farm hand, quarryman, roadmender and mine worker – yet in that time also managed to pen an impressive collection of poetry, sometimes having to dictate verses to fellow workers because of his failing eyesight.

A.B. "BANJO" PATERSON 1864–1941

One of Australia's most loved poets, Banjo Paterson wrote the majority of his poetry before the age of 40. He also had a successful legal career, was a war correspondent during the Boer War, went on to be a journalist in Australia and later lent his knowledge of horsemanship to the First World War effort, rising to the rank of major. He is best known for such works as *Waltzing Matilda* and *The Man from Snowy River*.

A.B. "BANJO" PATERSON

from *Australian Scenery*

A land of sombre, silent hills, where mountain cattle go
By twisted tracks, on sidelings steep, where giant gum trees grow
And the wind replies, in the river oaks, to the song of the stream below.

. . .

A land where silence lies so deep that sound itself is dead
And a gaunt grey bird, like a homeless soul, drifts, noiseless, overhead
And the world's great story is left untold, and the message is left unsaid.

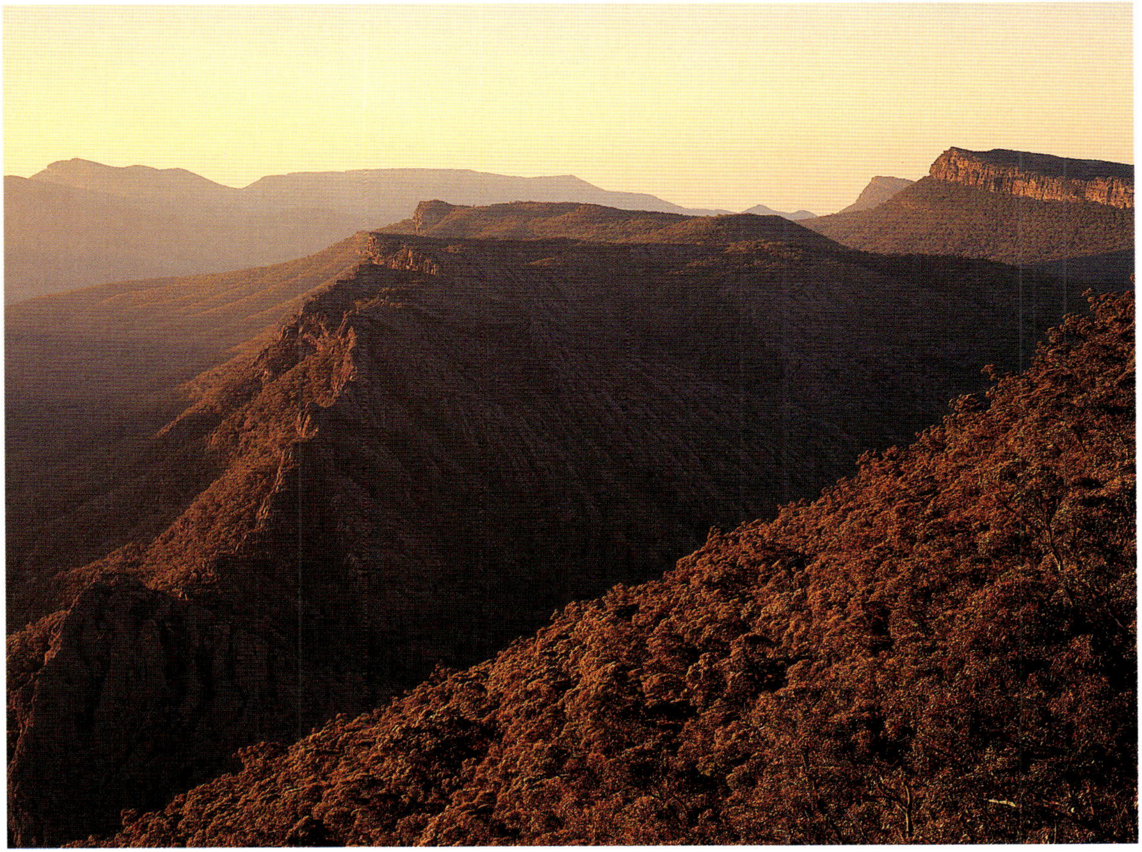

The Grampians, Victoria

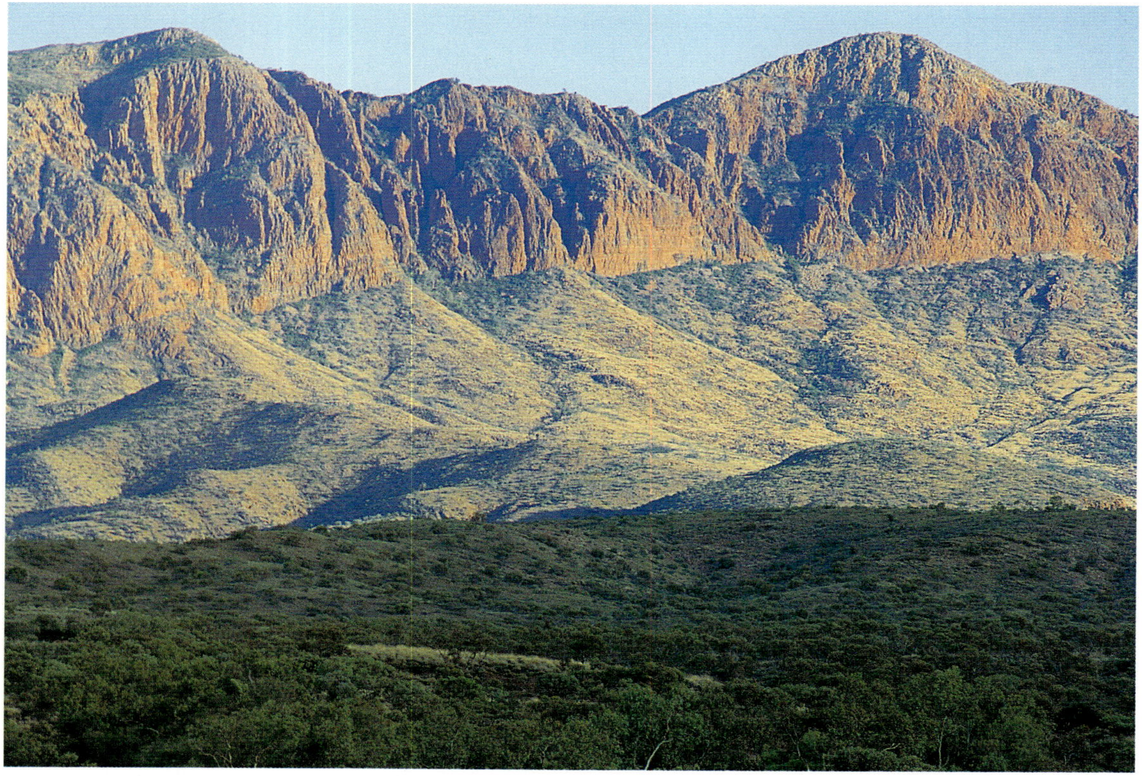

Mt Sonder, Northern Territory

George Essex Evans

from *Alone*

The purple hills rise far behind,
Before me spreads the plain,
The tall grass shakes beneath the wind
Like surges on the main.
Thin mists have girt each low hill's crest,
The hot sun swims in cloudless blue,
A mirage gathers in the West
And trembles into view

Henry Lawson

from *The Blue Mountains*

Now in the west the colours change,
The blue with crimson blending;
Behind the far Dividing Range
The sun is fast descending.

And mellowed day comes o'er the place,
And softens ragged edges;
The rising moon's great placid face
Looks gravely o'er the ledges.

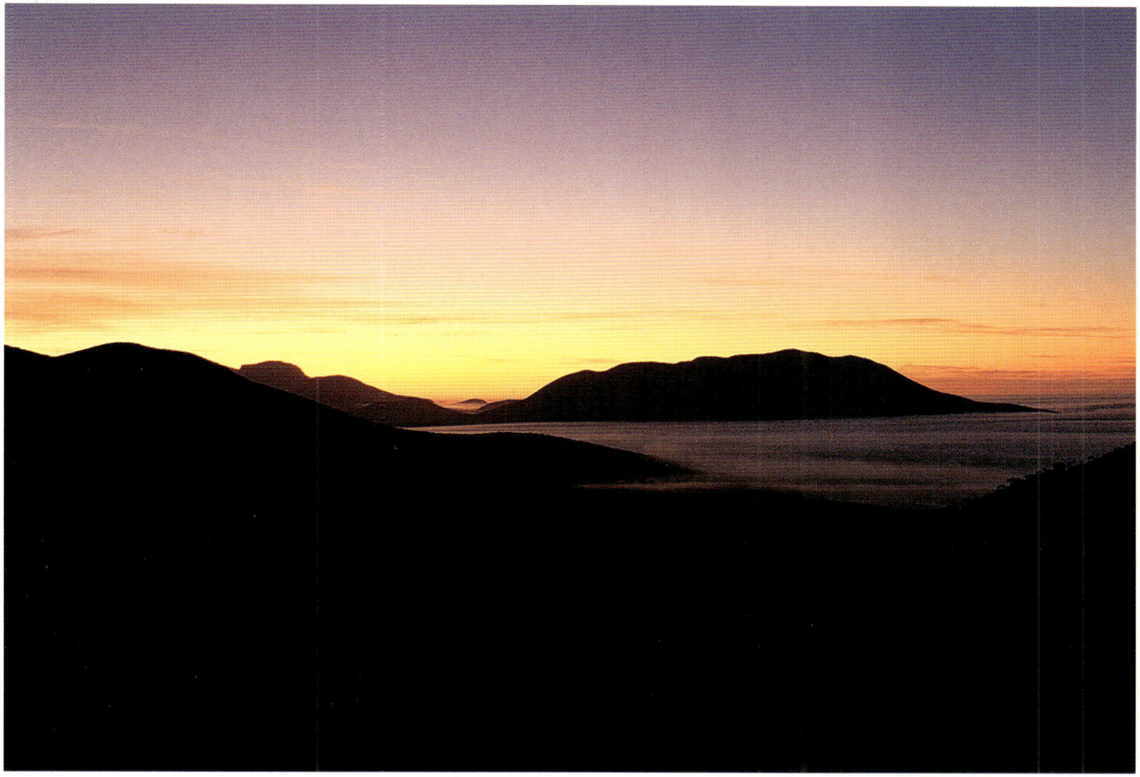

Stirling Range, Western Australia

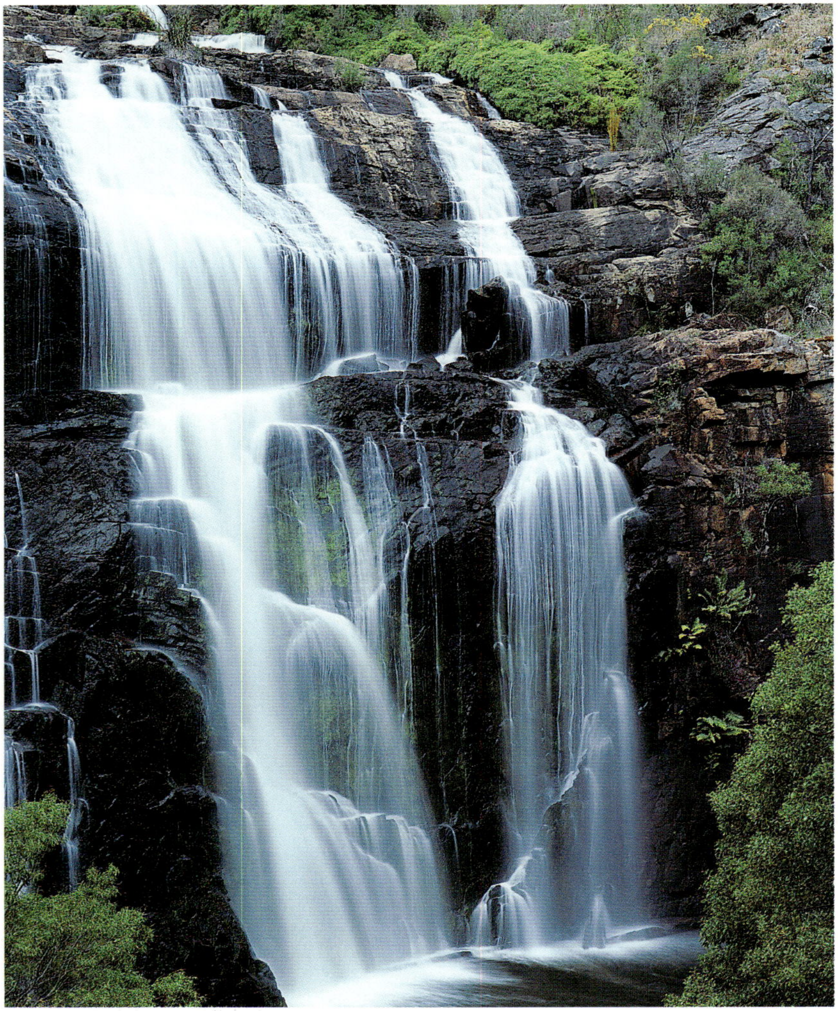

The Grampians, Victoria

Henry Kendall

from *Mountains*

Stately mountains, high and hoary, piled with blocks of amber cloud,
Where the fading twilight lingers, when the winds are wailing loud;
Grand old mountains, overbeetling brawling brooks and deep ravines,
Where the moonshine, pale and mournful, flows on rocks and evergreens.

CHARLES HARPUR

from *The Creek of the Four Graves*

Before them, thus extended, wilder grew
The scene each moment – and more wilder.
For when the sun was all but sunk below
Those barrier mountains, – in the breeze that o'er
Their rough enormous backs deep fleeced with wood
Came whispering down, the wide upslanting sea
Of fanning leaves in the descending rays
Danced interdazzlingly, as if the trees
That bore them, were all thrilling, – tingling all
Even to the roots for very happiness;
So prompted from within, so sentient, seemed
The bright quick motion – wildly beautiful.

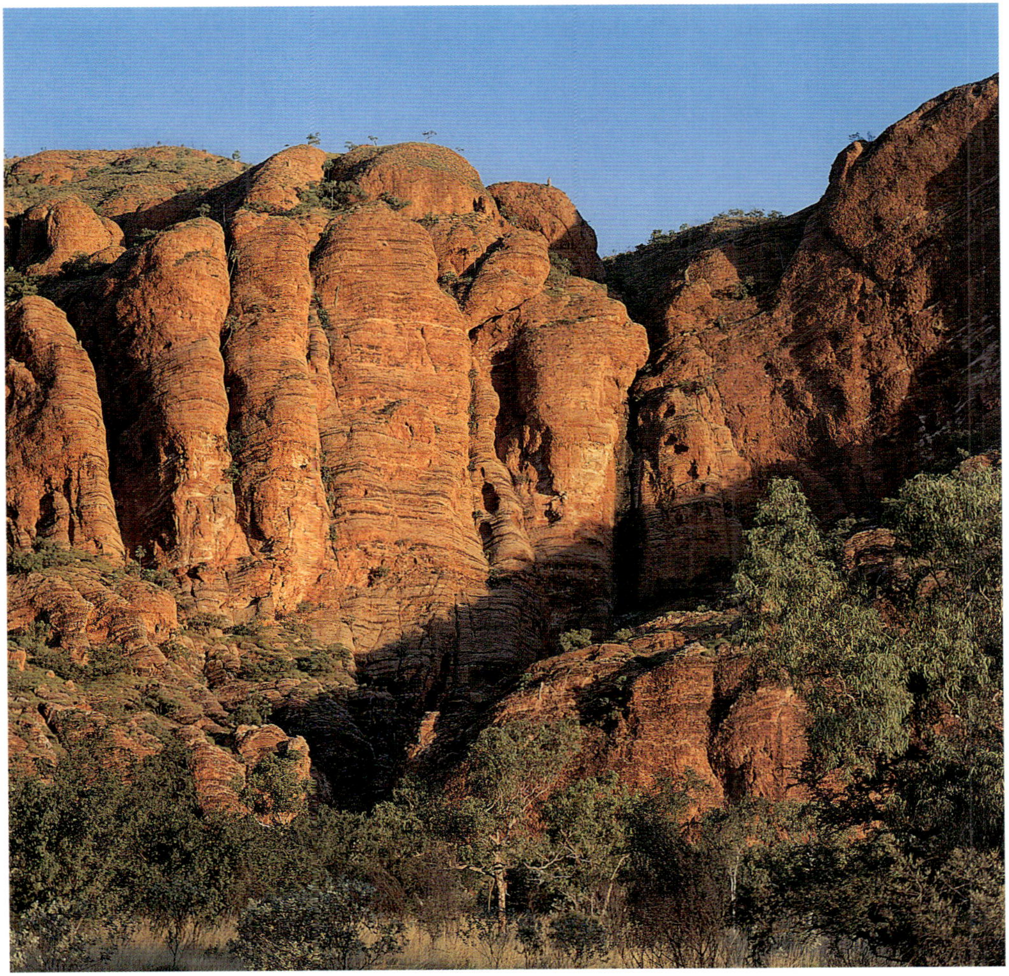

Bungle Bungle Range, Western Australia

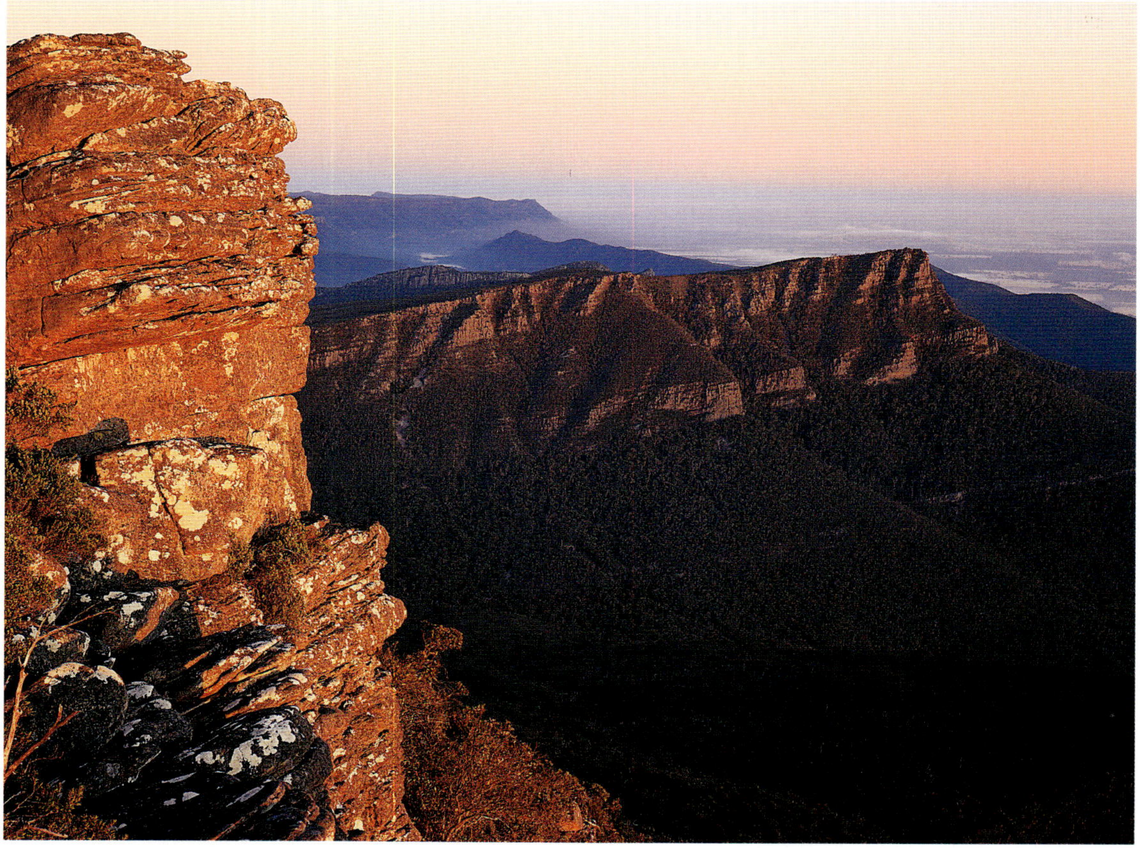

The Grampians, Victoria

John Shaw Neilson

from *The Winter Sundown*

The highlands, the hilltops,
    They make the heart bare,
Burned out with wishing for
    That country out there.

George Essex Evans

from *Kara*

Chequered with sunshine and shade – the umbrage of white clouds in motion –
Rearing their summits to Heaven, broken like waves on their strands,
Northward and southward and seaward the mountains arise from the ocean –

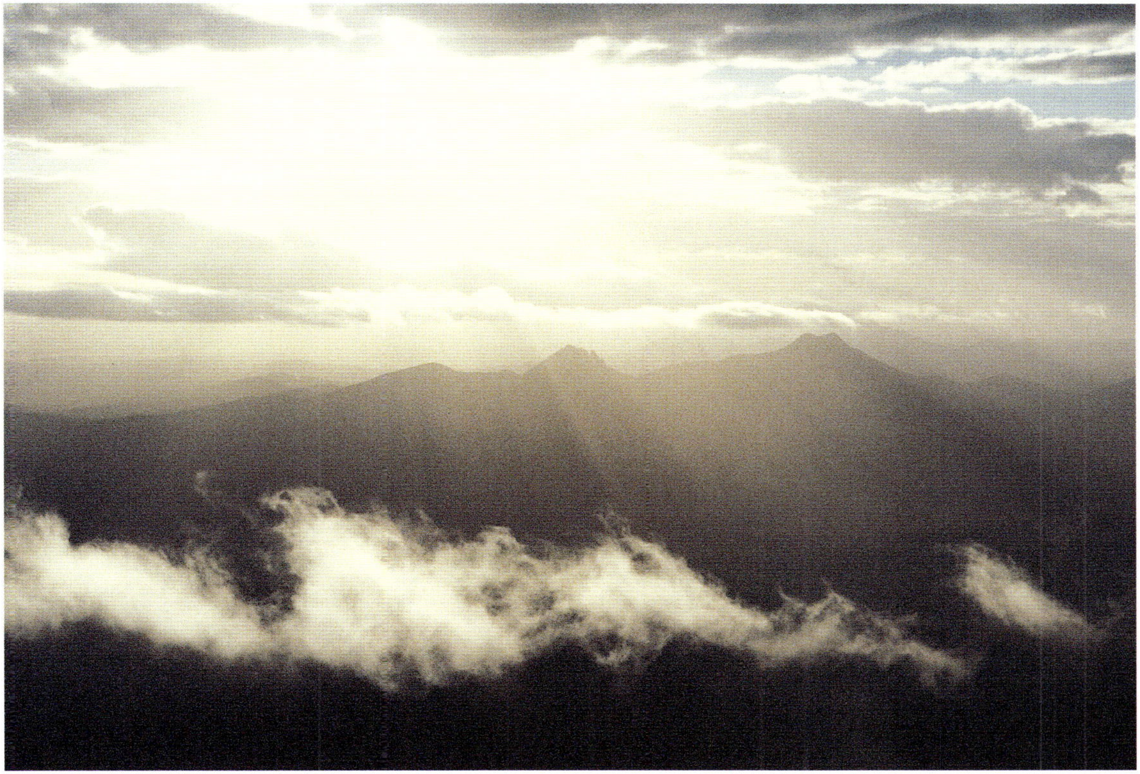

Stirling Range, Western Australia

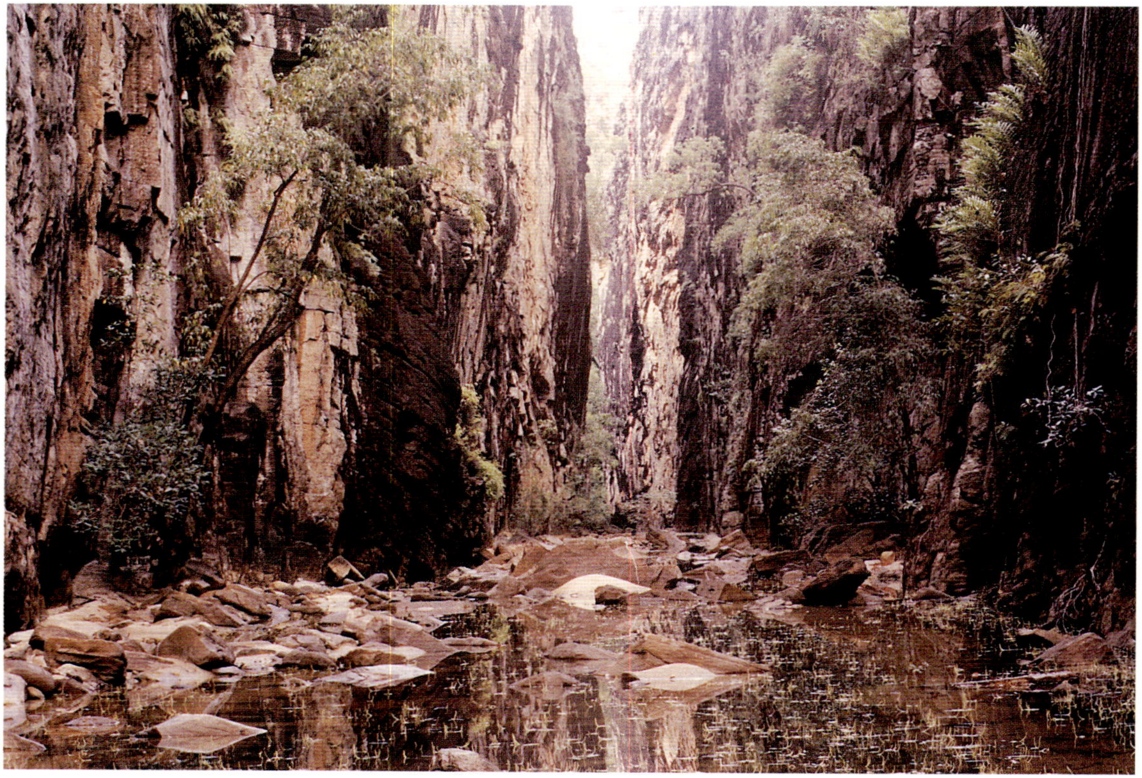

Kakadu National Park, Northern Territory

Ada Cambridge

from *Practising the Anthem*

Clear through the silence, from a reedy pool
    The curlew's whistle thrills;
A lonely mopoke sorrowfully cries
    From the far-folding hills.

A.B. "BANJO" PATERSON

from *Brumby's Run*

But when the dawn makes pink the sky
And steals along the plain,
The Brumby horses turn and fly
Towards the hills again.

The traveller by the mountain track
May hear their hoofbeats pass,
And catch a glimpse of brown and black,
Dim shadows on the grass.

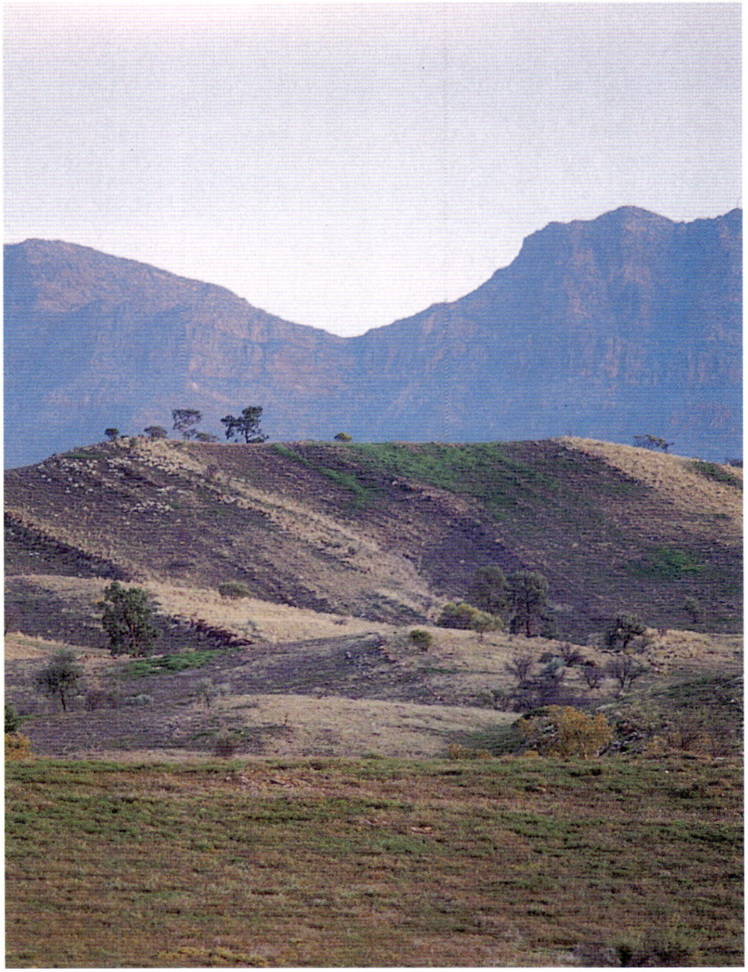

Flinders Ranges, South Australia

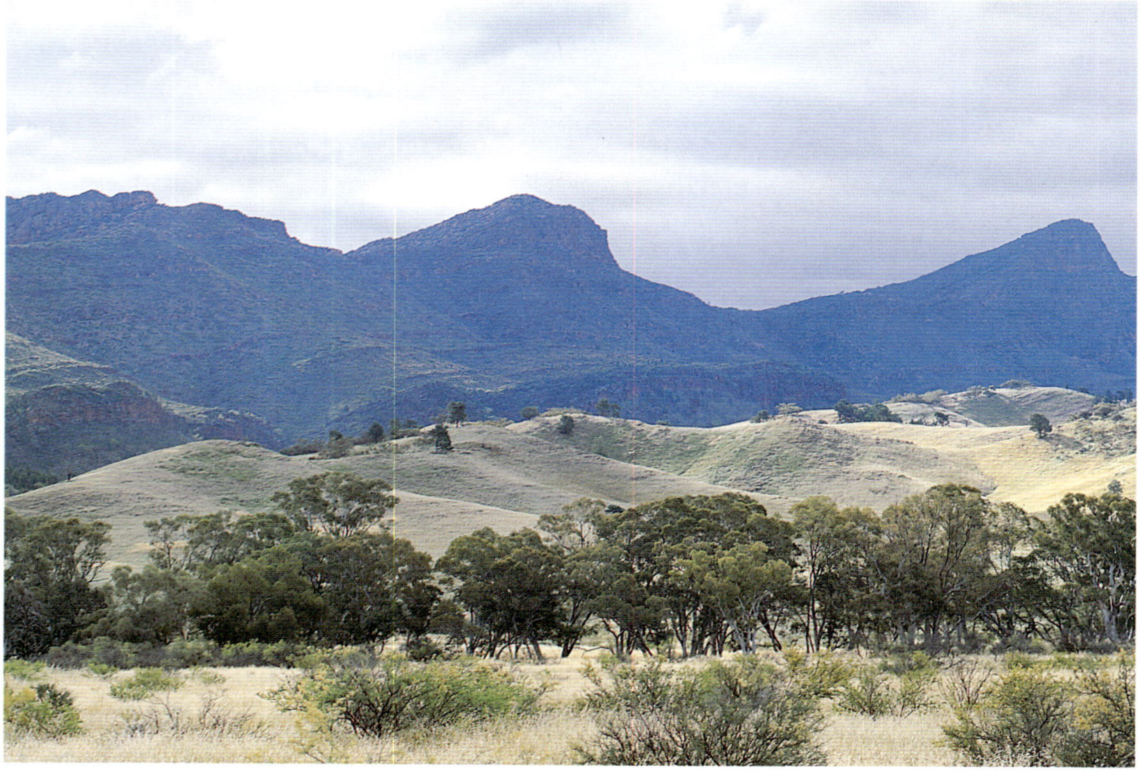

Flinders Ranges, South Australia

Henry Lawson

from *Reedy River*

And grassy slopes rise gently
To ridges long and low,
Where groves of wattle flourish
And native bluebells grow.

HENRY KENDALL

from A *Mountain Spring*

Peace hath an altar there. The sounding feet
Of thunder and the 'wildering wings of rain
Against fire-rifted summits flash and beat,
And through grey upper gorges swoop and strain;
But round that hallowed mountain-spring remain,
Year after year, the days of tender heat,
And gracious nights, whose lips with flowers are sweet,
And filtered lights, and lutes of soft refrain.

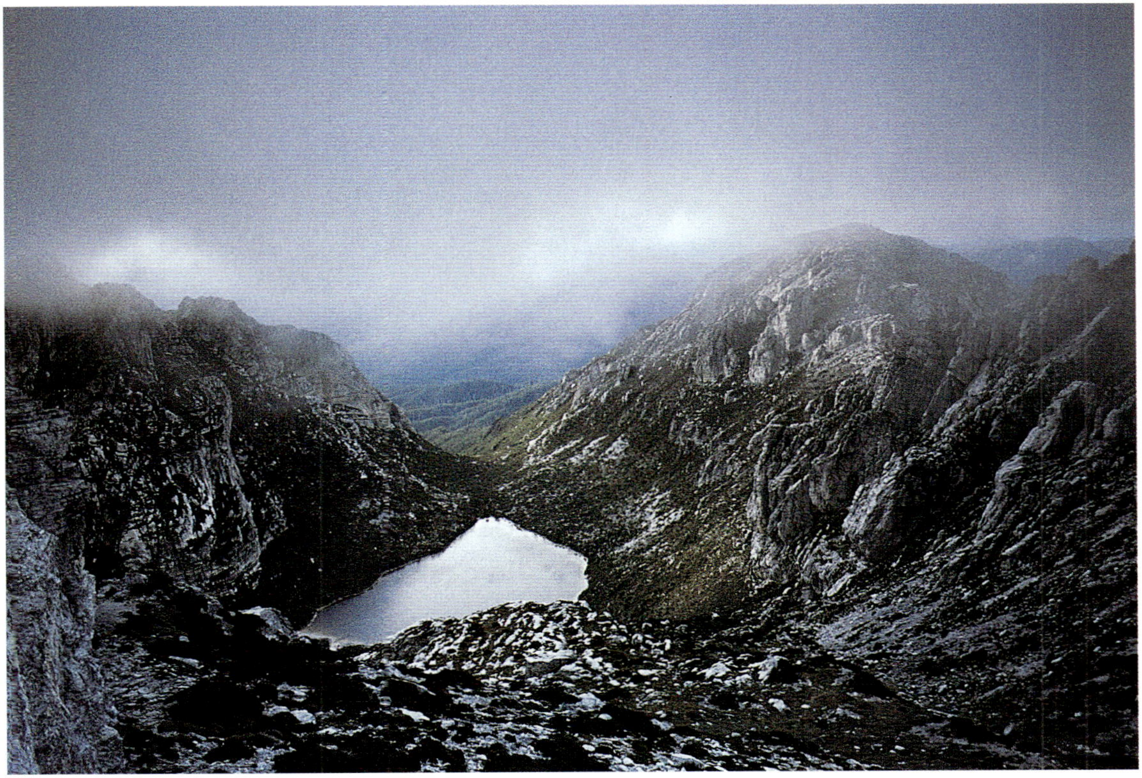

Frenchmans Cap, Tasmania

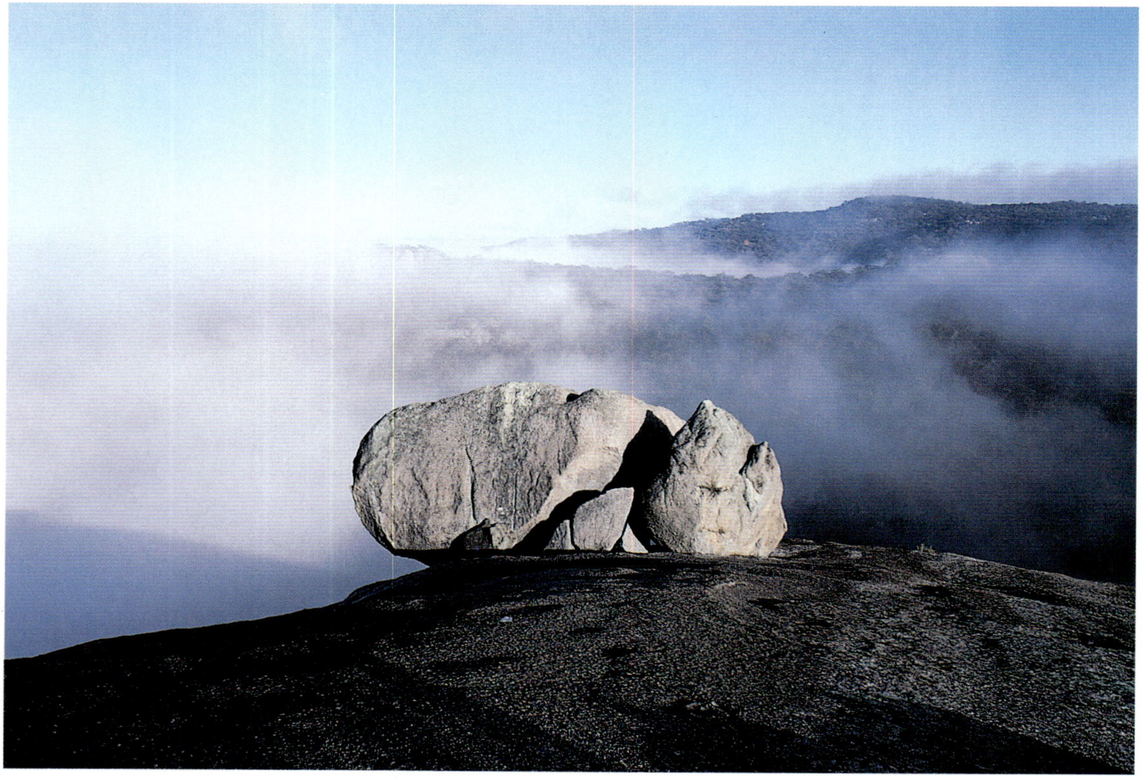

Girraween National Park, Queensland

Emilie Manning Heron

("Australie")

from *Bodalla*

The very air of all this peaceful land
Is soft and still, for sheltering mountains rise,
And, glooming blue and dark with varying shade,
Shut out the blighting winds, that restless blow
Yet cannot pass the tree-clad ramparts high;
While all the moisture streaming from the earth,
Held in, though rising, turns to dewy mist
And veils th' enclosing hills in sweet revenge

George Essex Evans

from A *Medley*

Soft and tender is the fancy which thro' all my being thrills,
When the chequered lights and shadows play upon the purple hills;
When the burning skies to westward fade to floods of amber light,
And the lemon tints of sunset melt into the dusks of night.

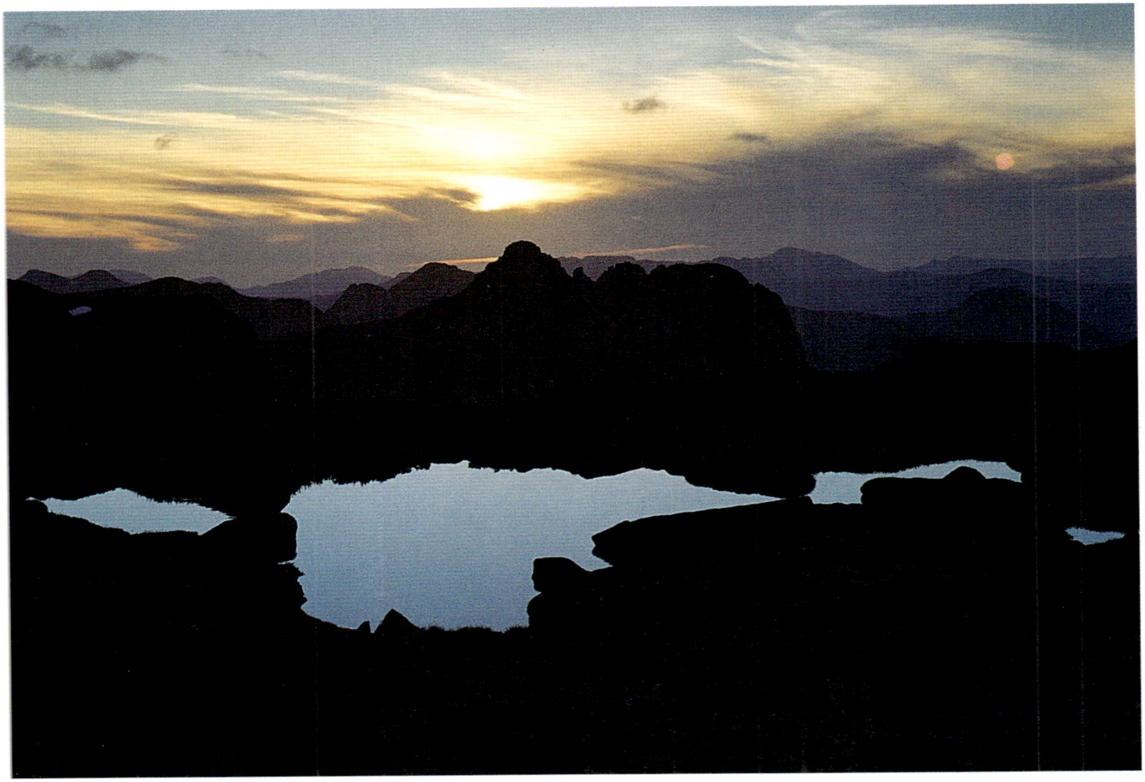

Cradle Mountain, Tasmania

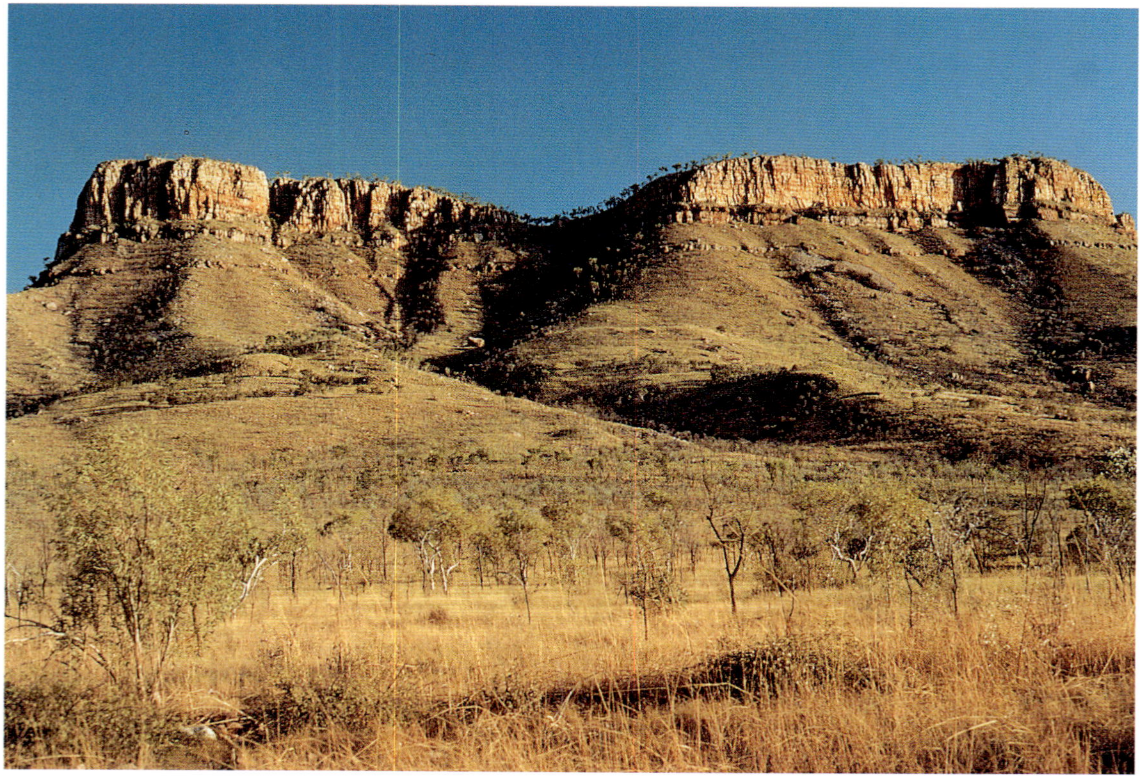

Hamersley Range, Western Australia

Adam Lindsay Gordon

from *De Te*

A burning glass of burnish'd brass,
The calm sea caught the noontide rays,
And sunny slopes of golden grass
And wastes of weed-flower seem to blaze.
Beyond the shining silver-greys,
Beyond the shades of denser bloom,
The sky-line girt with glowing haze,
The farthest faintest forest gloom,
And the everlasting hills that loom.

George Essex Evans

from *The Secret Key*

Or, where the streaming mist's white rollers climb
The dark ravine and precipice sublime –
A filmy sea that twines and intertwines
Wreathes the low hills, and veils the mighty lines
Of sovran mountains, crimsoned and aglow
In crystal pomp, crested with jewelled snow

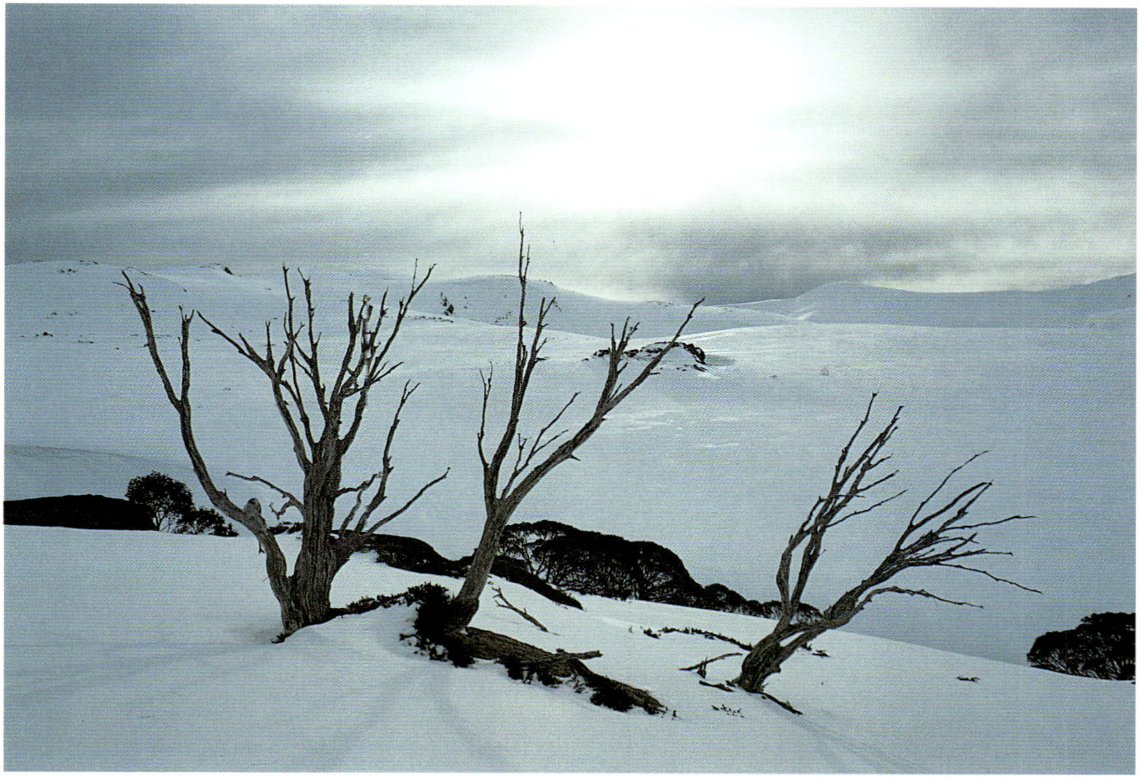

Charlottes Pass, New South Wales

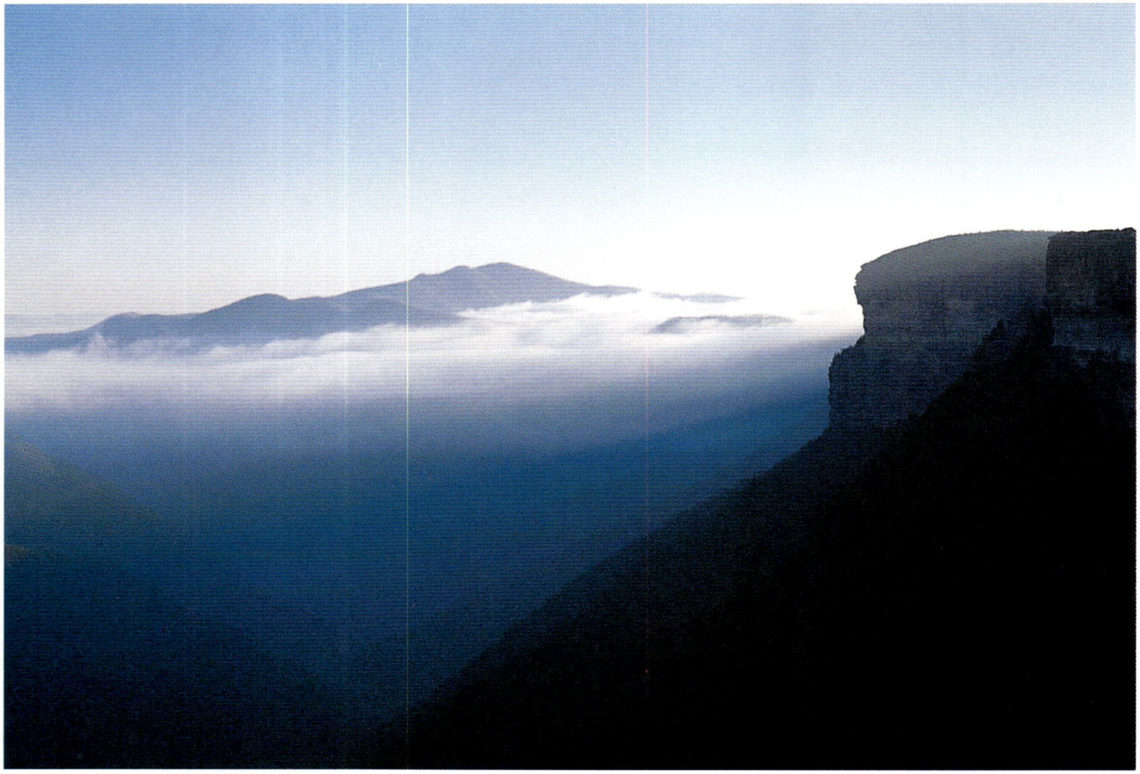

Kanangra Walls, New South Wales

VICTOR DALEY

from *Fragments*

Fade off the ridges, rosy light,
Fade slowly from the last grey height,
And leave no gloomy cloud to grieve
The heart of this enchanted eve!

George Essex Evans
from *The Land of the Dawning*

Dark rose her shore in seas of amethyst
By tropic breezes kissed,
A summer land in watery wastes forlorn,
Her ranges floating in the snow white mist
And gold of early morn.

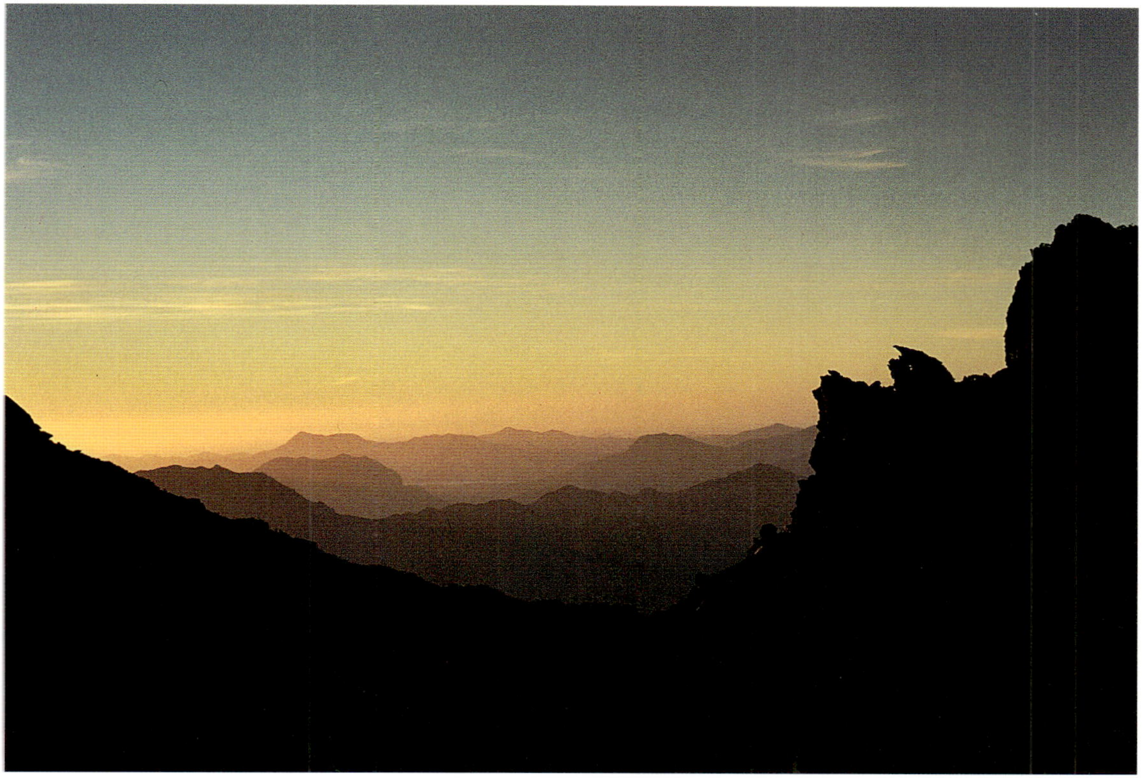

South West National Park, Tasmania

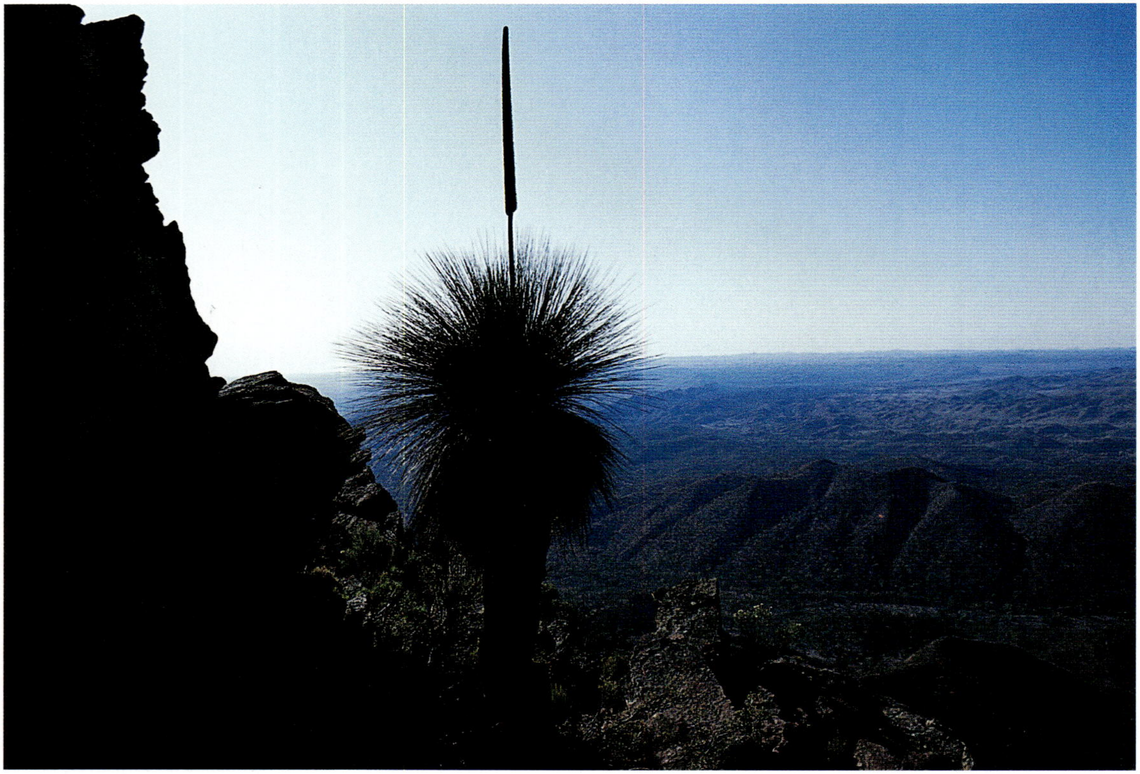

Wilpena Pound, South Australia

GEORGE ESSEX EVANS
from *The Land of the Dawning*

In feathery billows of her grassy seas
Some lonely mountain stretched its capes of blue;
Only the heavens above her and the breeze
Her secrets knew.

George Essex Evans
from *The Land of the Dawning*

Where the wild grass grew rank on slopes forlorn
Rise fields of yellow corn,
And purple lucerne-bloom makes sweet the air;
The sullen mountain, lost in mists of morn,
Its golden heart lays bare.

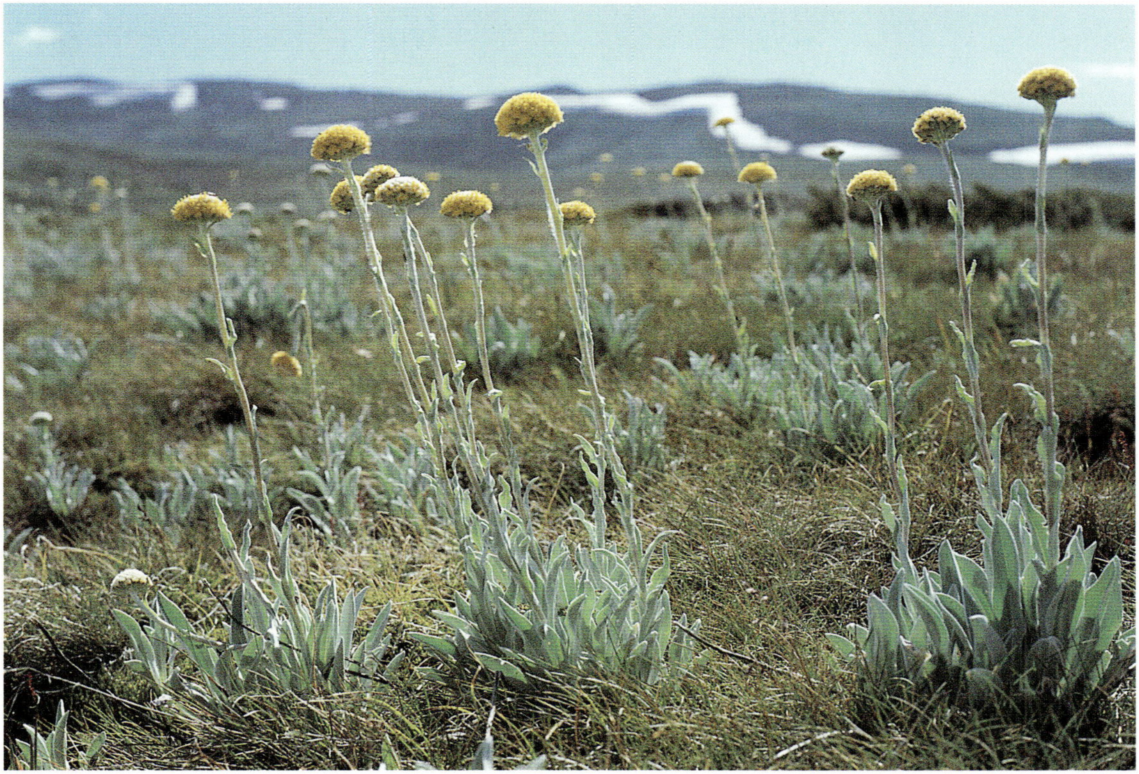

Mt Kosciusko, New South Wales

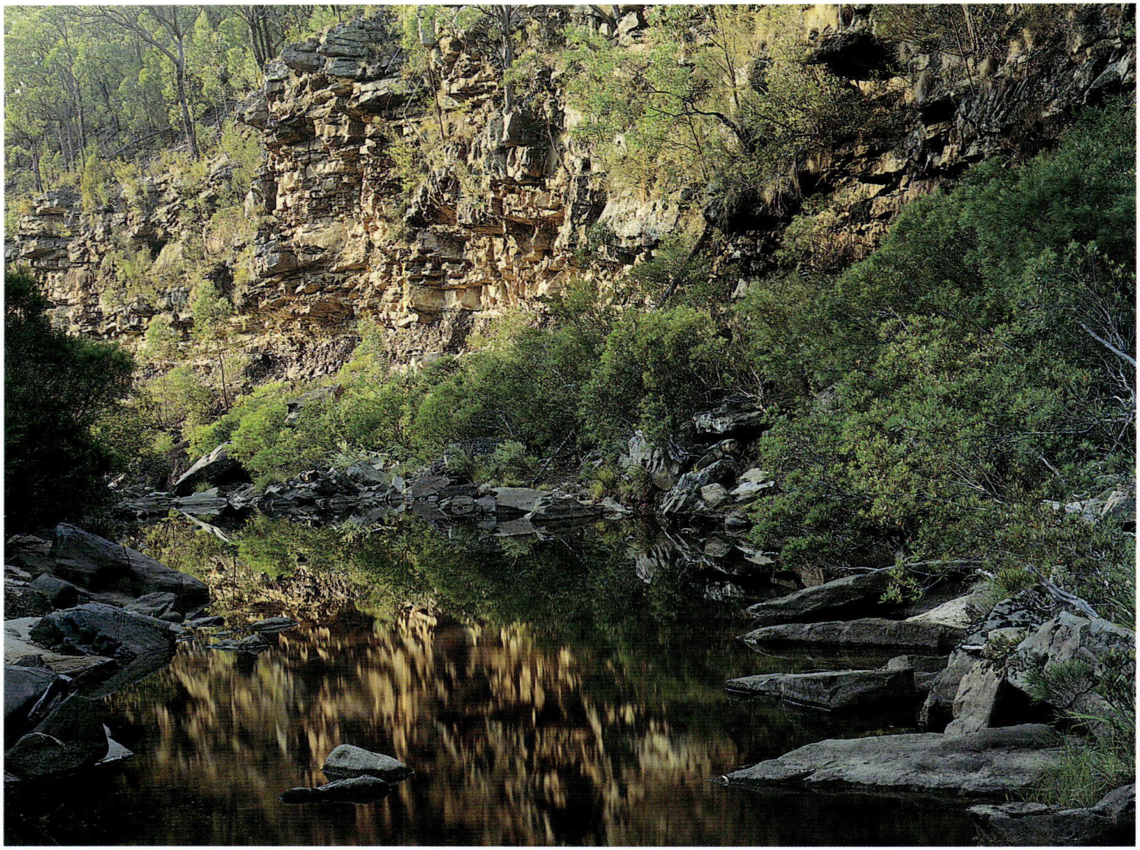

Snowy River Gorge, Victoria

A.B. "Banjo" Paterson

from *The Man from Snowy River*

"He hails from Snowy River, up by Kosciusko's side,
Where the hills are twice as steep and twice as rough,
Where a horse's hoofs strike firelight from the flint stones every stride,
The man that holds his own is good enough.
And the Snowy River riders on the mountains make their home,
Where the river runs those giant hills between;
I have seen full many horsemen since I first commenced to roam,
But nowhere yet such horsemen have I seen."

Henry Lawson

from *Rain in the Mountains*

The valley's full of misty clouds,
Its tinted beauty drowning,
Tree-tops are veiled in fleecy shrouds,
And mountain fronts are frowning.

The mist is hanging like a pall
Above the granite ledges,
And many a silvery waterfall
Leaps o'er the valley's edges.

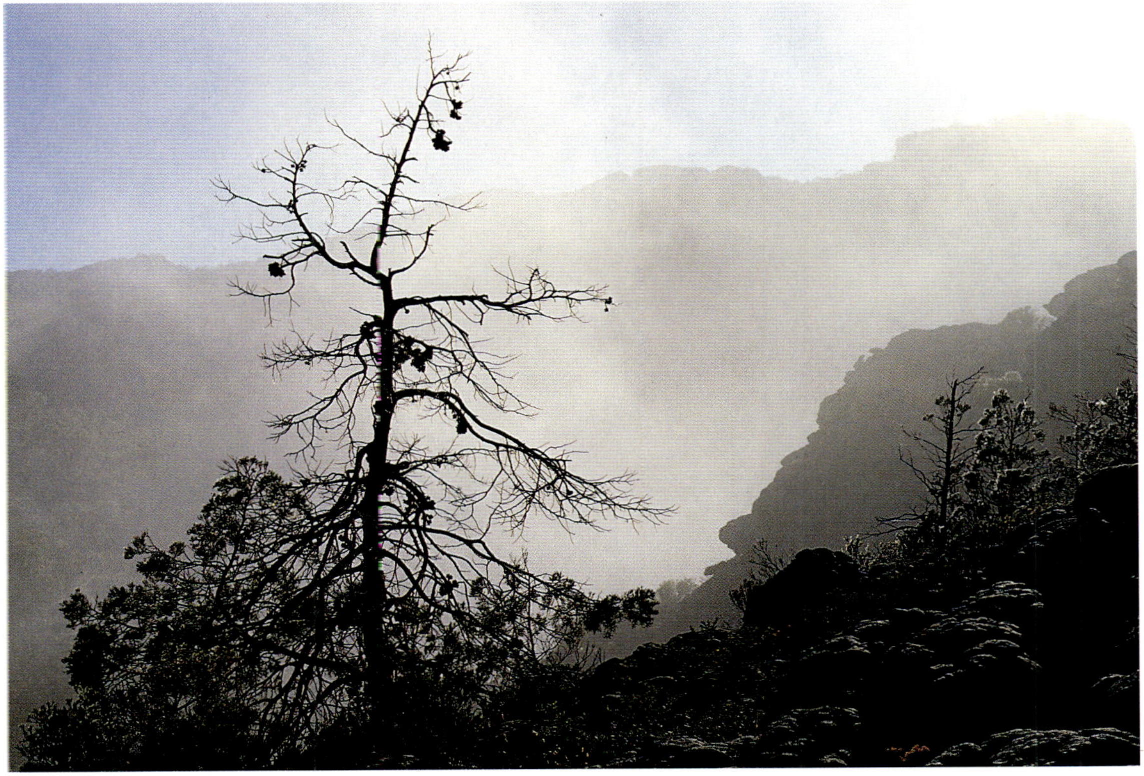

The Grampians, Victoria

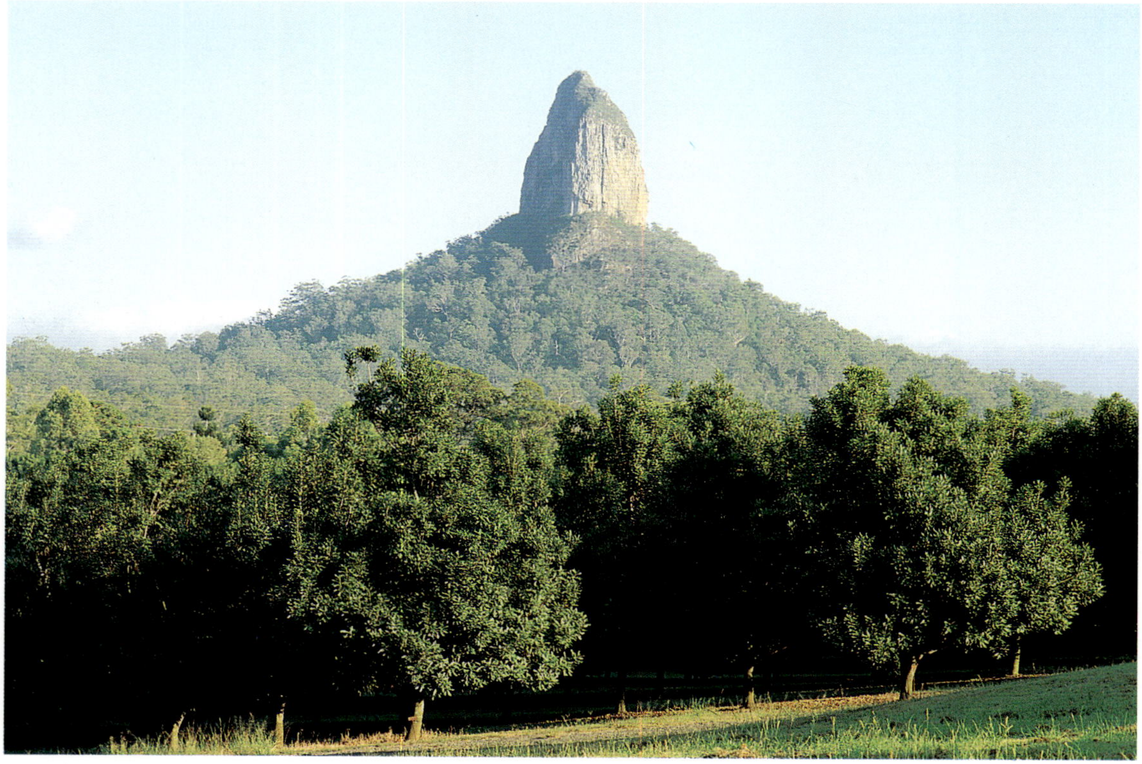

Glass House Mountains, Queensland

Henry Kendall

from *Mountains*

Rifted mountains, clad with forests, girded round by gleaming pines,
Where the morning, like an angel, robed in golden splendour shines;
Shimmering mountains, throwing downward on the slopes a mazy glare
Where the noonday glory sails through gulfs of calm and glittering air

George Essex Evans

from *Toowoomba*

Dark purple, chased with sudden gloom and glory,
Like waves in wild unrest,
Low-wooded billows and steep summits hoary,
Ridge, slope, and mountain crest

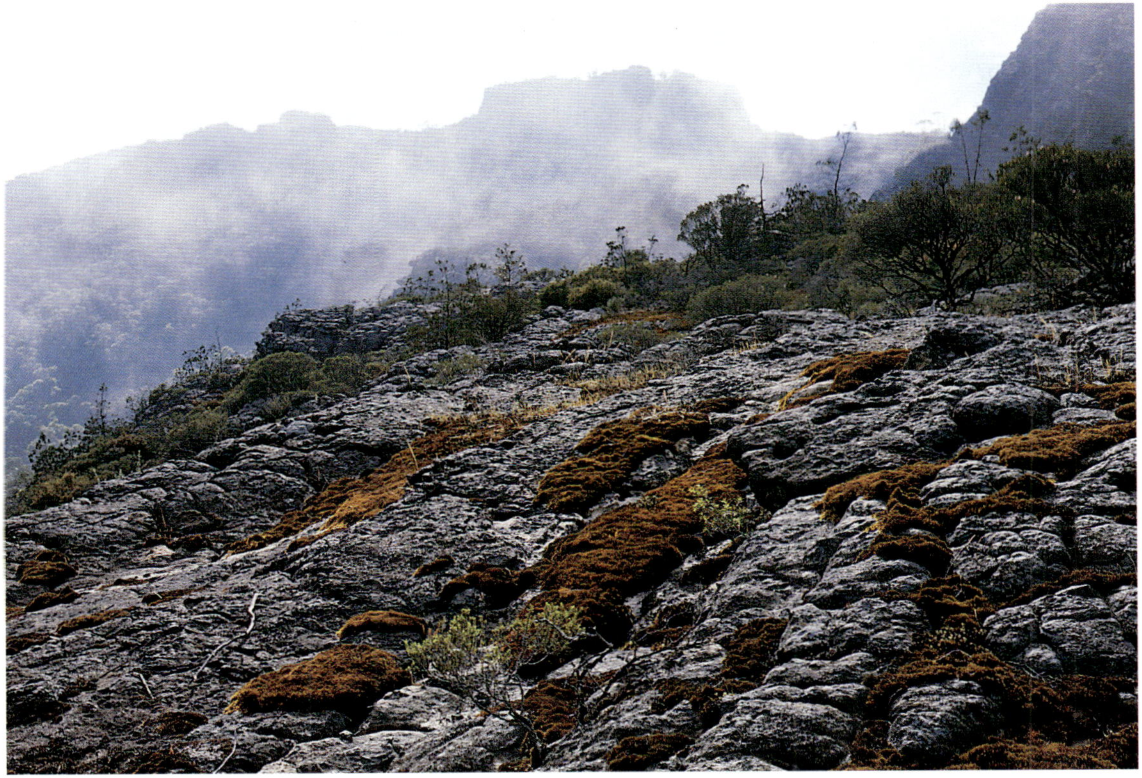

The Grampians, Victoria

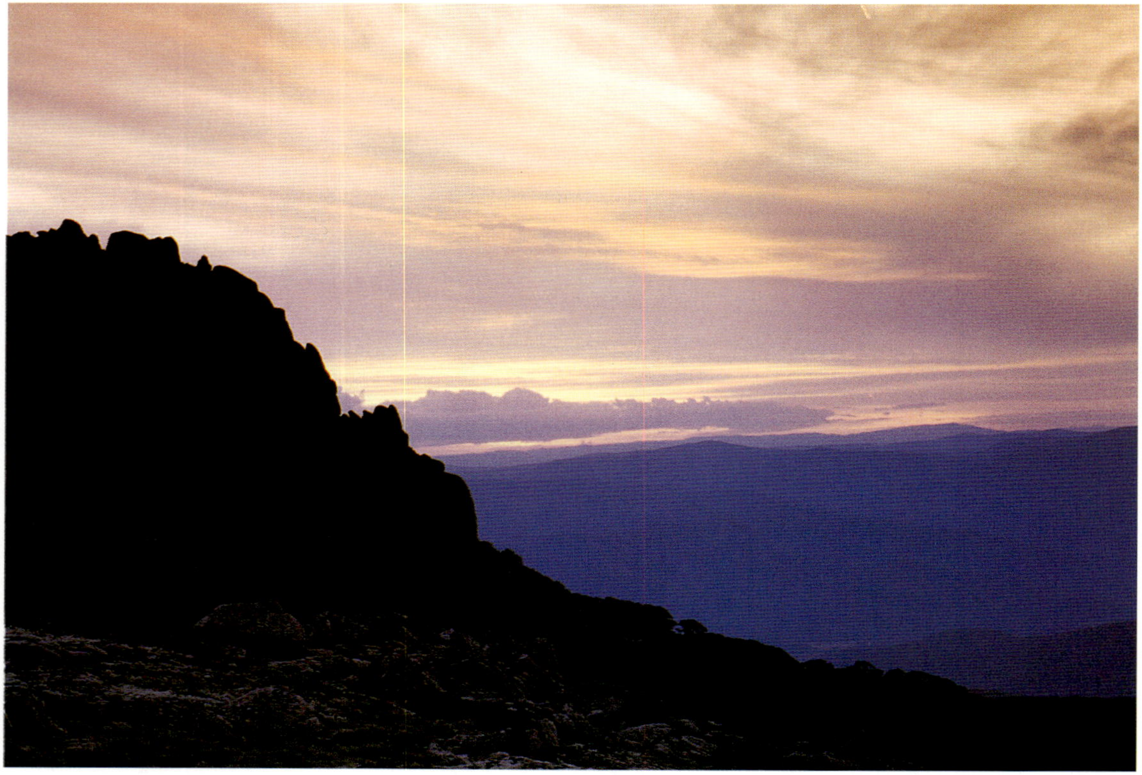

Kosciusko National Park, New South Wales

Christopher Brennan

from *Poems* (1913)

And sudden, 'twixt a sun and sun,
the veil of dreaming is withdrawn:
lo, our disrupt dominion
and mountains solemn in the dawn

Victor Daley

from *Fragments*

The shadows gather over all,
The valley, and the mountains old;
Shadow on shadow fast they fall
On glooming green and waning gold

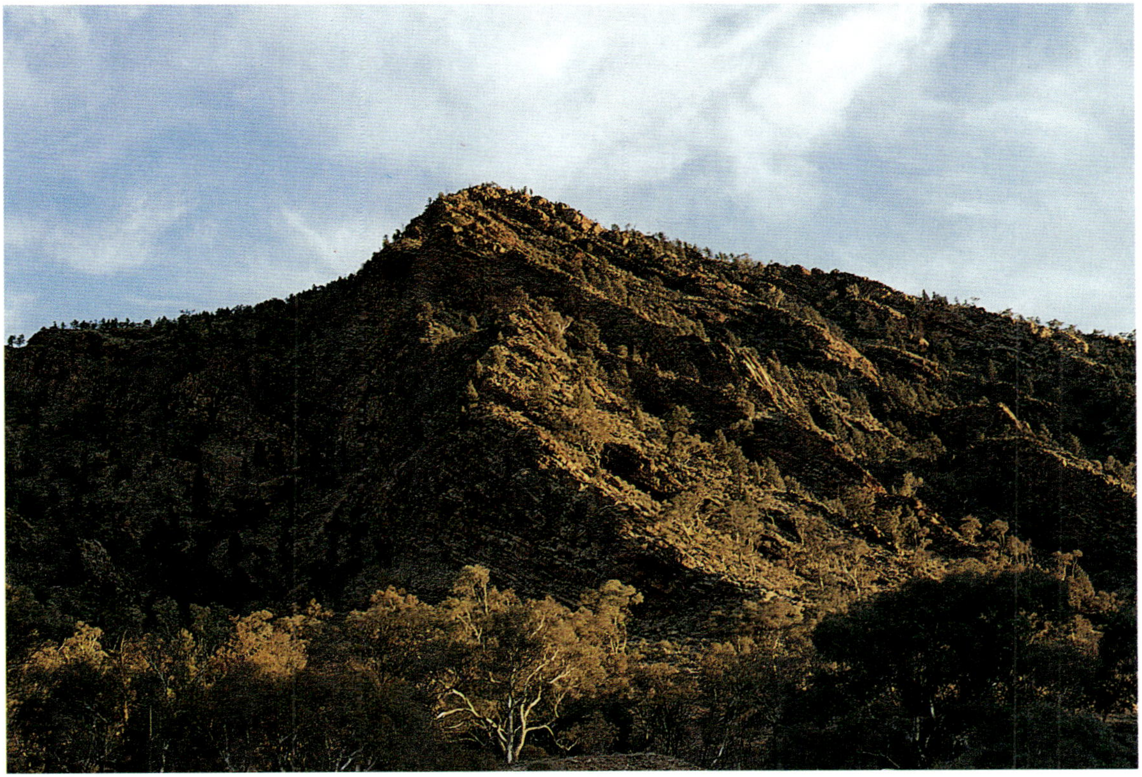

Brachina, South Australia

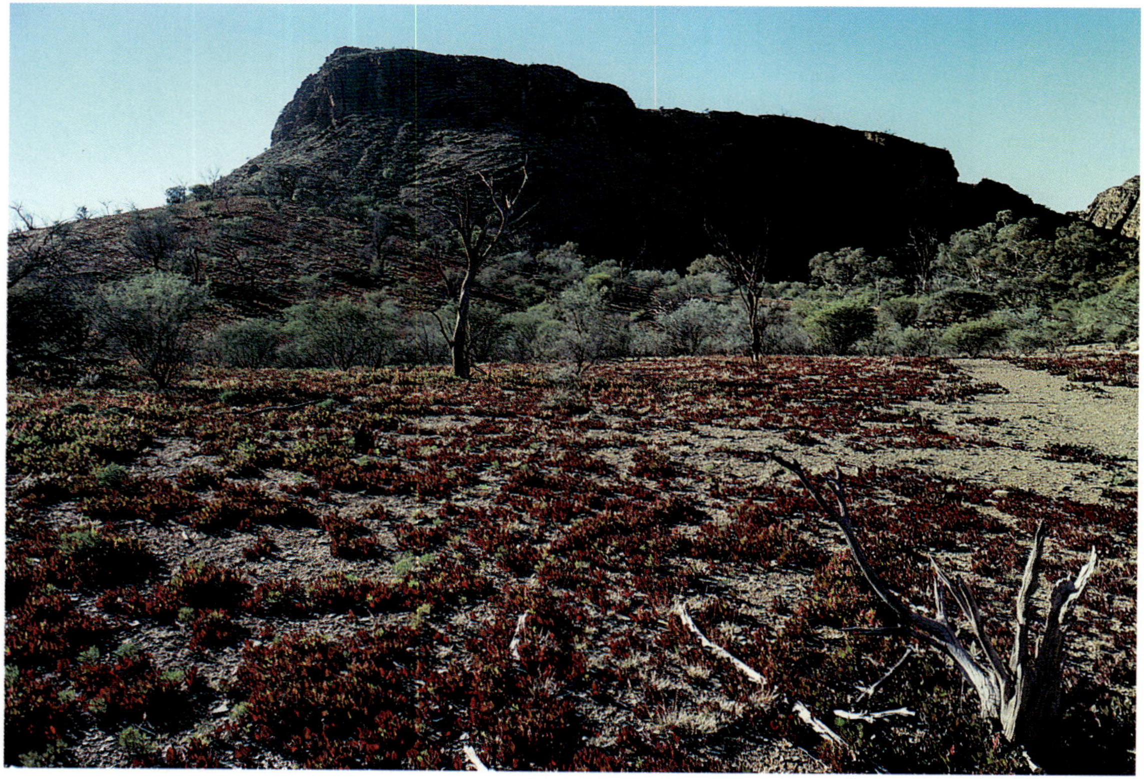

Flinders Ranges, South Australia

Louisa Lawson

from *In Memory of* R.E.H.

Again we climb the mountain spur where sober she-oaks sigh,
To cull a wealth of wattle bloom, and seek the purple vine
That round the rugged ironbarks in velvet circles twine.

George Essex Evans

from A *Pastoral*

Darkly, like an armèd host
Seen afar against the blue,
Rise the hills, and yellow grey
Sleeps the plain in cove and bay,
Like a shining sea that dreams
Round a silent coast.

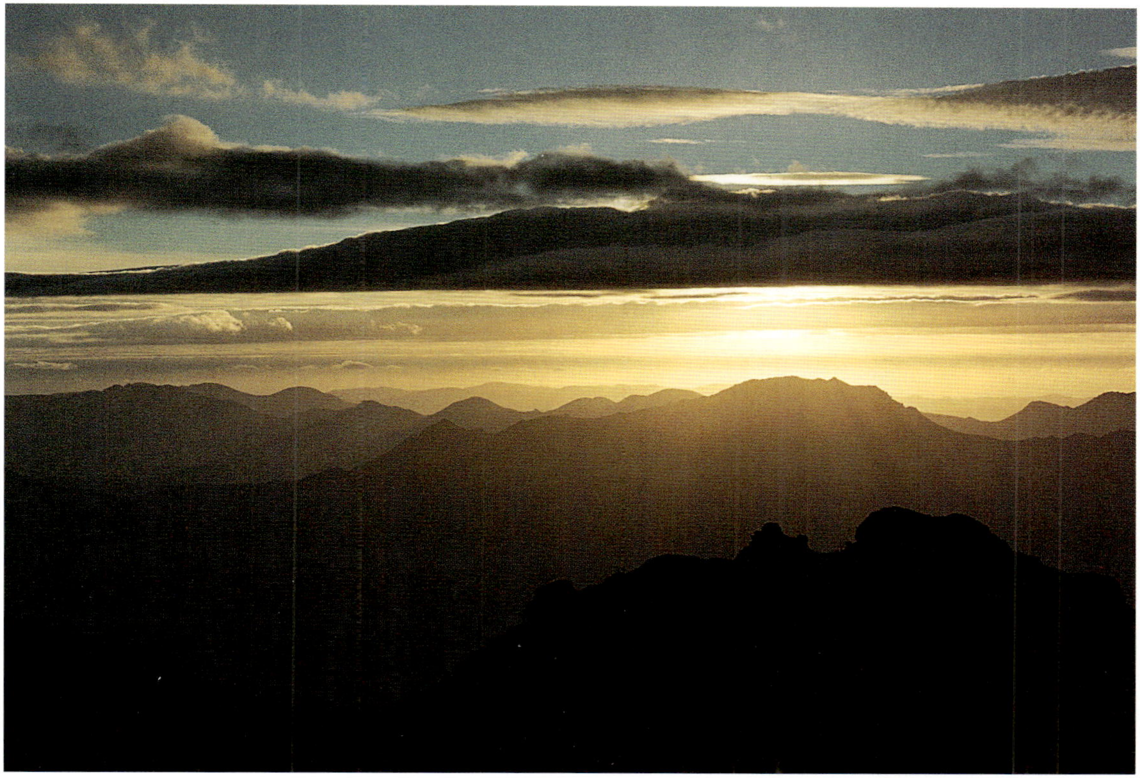

South West National Park, Tasmania

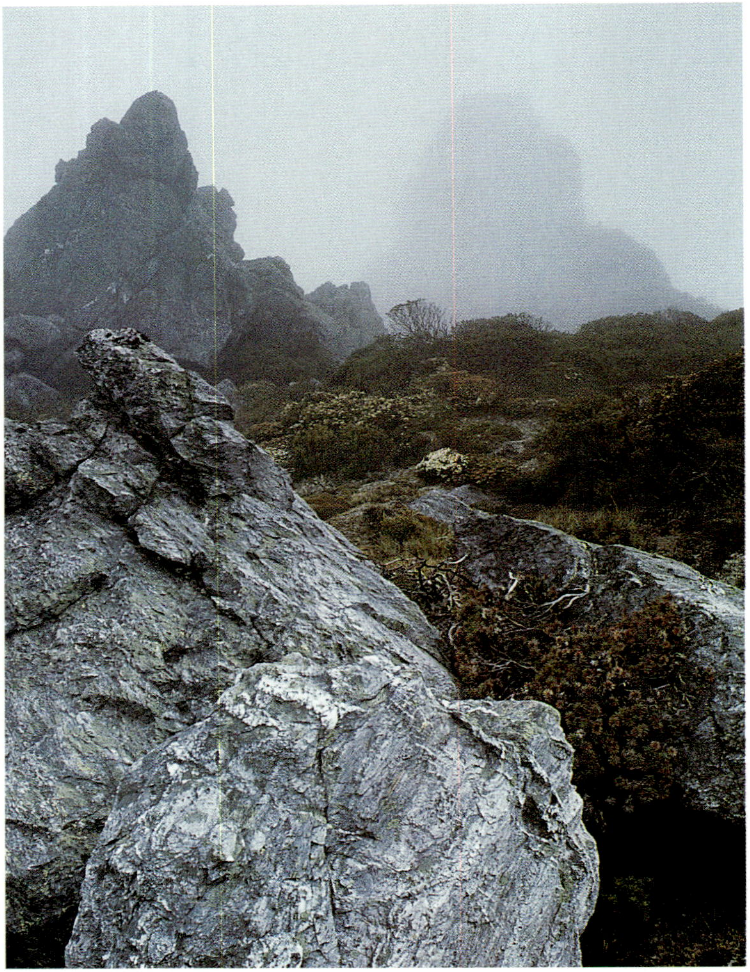

FEDERATION PEAK, TASMANIA

George Essex Evans

from *Kara*

High as an eagle's nest, crowning a summit storm-beaten and hoary,
Framed in a setting of green which sombre tints deepen and tone,
Gleam all the station's white roofs, refracting the Summer god's glory:
Ribbons of silvery light surmounting grey masses of stone.

George Essex Evans

from *An Echo*

When the crimson-tinted sunlight sinks and pales in waning rays,
And like rush of many waters, come the thoughts of other days;
Till the creeping mists grow deeper and the evening air is still
With the awe of solemn shadows hanging darkly on the hill;
Till with wide and rapid pinions sweeps the Spirit of the Night,
And our thoughts are carried onwards in the current of its flight,
Through the wreathing mists of darkness where the midnight reigns alone
From the regions of the Finite to the bars of the Unknown.

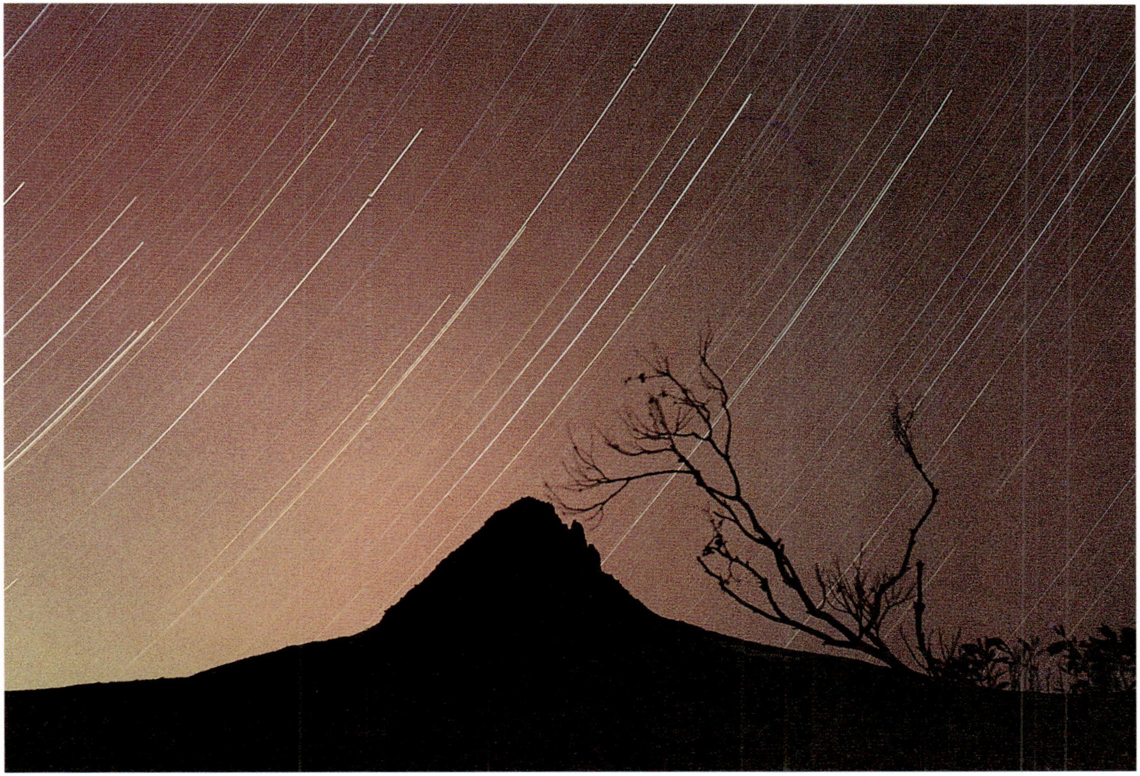

Barn Bluff, Tasmania

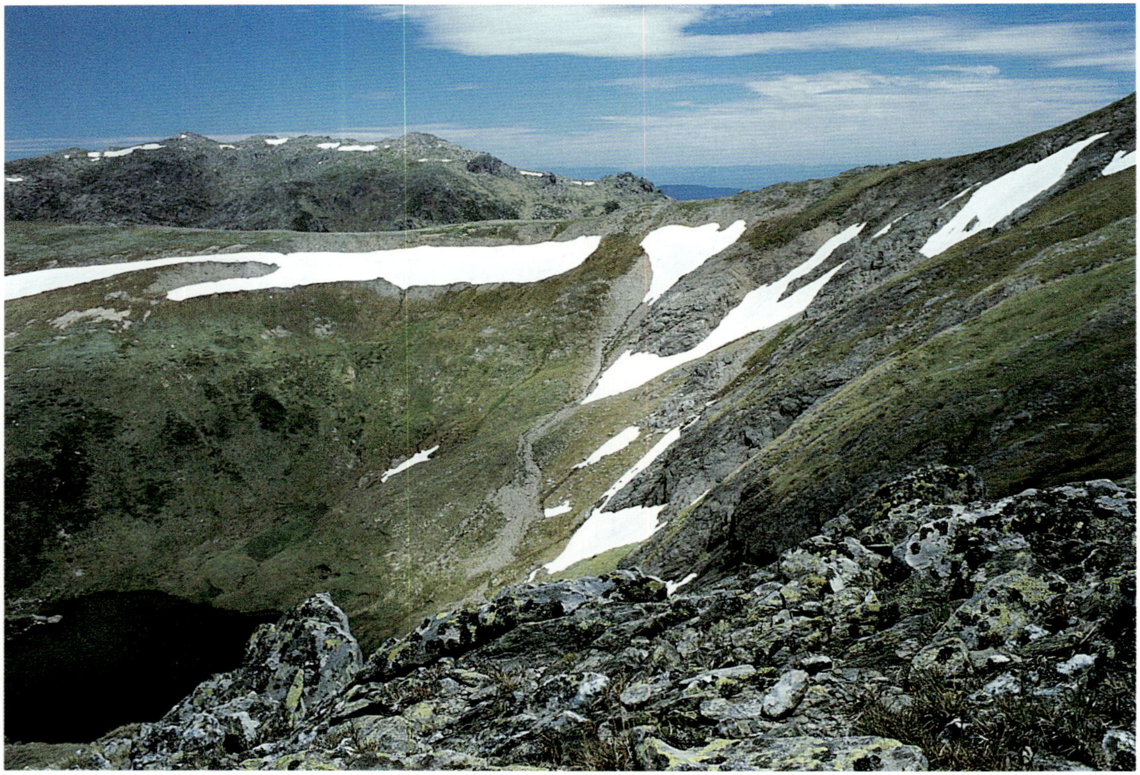

Club Lake, New South Wales

GEORGE ESSEX EVANS

from A *Medley*

Eastward in the skies of morning rosy tinges streak the grey
Bars of crimson change to golden – glittr'ing heralds of
the day,
Like a blood red shield uprising swims the sun in palest blue,
Crowns the hills with crests of splendour, flashes on the
trembling dew

Principal Photography

JOHN MEIER is influenced by the painters and the composers of the romantic period. He endeavours to portray the spiritual qualities of Australia's wild places. John is a principal of Precious Planet Wilderness Photography His photographs can be found on pages 7, 12, 16, 20, 27, 31, 35, 36, 39, 40, 43, 44, 47, 51, 52, 55, 59, 60, 63 and 64.

Additional Photography

PETER JARVER is an award-winning landscape photographer best known for his images of the Northern Territory and its spectacular lightning displays. One of his photographs can be found on page 15.

CAROLYN JOHNS is based in Victoria and is best known for her film and portrait work. She is a founding member of Wildlight Photo Agency. One of her photographs can be found on page 48.

PHILIP QUIRK is a landscape photographer represented in many major public collections throughout Australia and is a founding member of Wildlight Photo Agency. His photographs can be found on pages 8, 11 and 28.

PETER SOLNESS is mostly known for his work documenting people in their environment. He has worked throughout Europe, Asia and Australia. His photographs can be found on pages 19, 24 and 32.

GRENVILLE TURNER photographs the Australian landscape and documents the environment and Australian wildlife. He is a founding member of Wildlight Photo Agency. His photographs can be found on pages 23 and 56.

Angus&Robertson
An imprint of HarperCollins*Publishers*, Australia

First published in Australia in 1995

HarperCollins*Publishers*
25 Ryde Road, Pymble, Sydney NSW 2073, Australia
31 View Road, Glenfield, Auckland 10, New Zealand
77–85 Fulham Palace Road, London W6 8JB, United Kingdom
Hazelton Lanes, 55 Avenue Road, Suite 2900, Toronto, Ontario M5R 3L2
and 1995 Markham Road, Scarborough, Ontario M1B 5M8, Canada
10 East 53rd Street, New York NY 10032, USA

National Library of Australia Cataloguing-in-Publication data:

The mountains: spirit of the land: a selection of classic
Australian poetry with contemporary Australian photography.

ISBN 0 207 18923 4

1. Australian poetry. 2. Australia – Poetry.
3. Australia – Pictorial works. I. Meier, John (John Richard).

A821.083294

Front cover photograph by John Meier

Printed in Australia by Griffin Colour

9 8 7 6 5 4 3 2 1
99 98 97 96